John Kember and Graeme Vinall

Sight-Reading 1

Déchiffrage pour la clarinette 1
Vom-Blatt-Spiel auf der Klarinette 1

A fresh approach / Nouvelle approche
Eine erfrischend neue Methode

ED 12834
ISMN M-2201-2381-8

www.schott-music.com

Mainz · London · Madrid · New York · Paris · Prague · Tokyo · Toronto
© 2006 Schott & Co. Ltd, London · Printed in Germany

ED 12834

British Library Cataloguing-in-Publication Data.
A catalogue record for this book is available from the British Library.
ISMN M-2201-2381-8
ISBN 1-902455-55-X

French translation: Agnès Ausseur
German translation: Ute Corleis
Design by www.adamhaystudio.com
Music setting by Willems Notensatz, Villingen-Schwenningen
Printed in Germany S&Co.8044

Contents

Sommaire/Inhalt

Preface

Clarinet Sight-Reading 1 aims to establish good practice and provide an early introduction to the essential skill of sight-reading.

Sight-reading given as 'homework' is of little value unless the result is heard by the teacher. Ideally, sight-reading in some form should become a regular part of a student's routine each time they get out their clarinet.

This book aims to establish the habit early in a student's clarinet playing. Of course, names of notes and time values need to be thoroughly known and understood, but equally sight-reading is helped by an awareness of shape and direction.

There are seven sections in this book, each of which gradually introduces new notes, rhythms, articulations, dynamics and Italian terms in a logical sequence, much as you would find in a beginner's clarinet tutor. The emphasis is on providing idiomatic tunes and structures rather than sterile sight-reading exercises. Each section concludes with three pupil-to-pupil duets and three accompanied solos which are intended to be a summary of the material introduced during that section.

Section 1 deals with the left-hand notes C – A, together with simple rhythms and time signatures. Melodic material emphasises movement by step, simple phrase structures, repeated notes and repeated melodic shapes (sequences).

Section 2 adds right hand B – G, slurs and some slightly more arpeggiated melodic shapes.

Section 3 extends the low register to include throat F♯, low B♭, throat B♭, low F and low E. Quavers and dotted crotchets are encountered for the first time together with the time signature of 5/4 and some easy changes of time signature. The key signatures of C, G and F major are introduced along with Italian terms and dynamics.

Section 4 sets up the often neglected compound time signatures of 6/8, 9/8 and 12/8, avoiding awkward rests and ties. Low register E♭ is used and there is limited use of accidentals. Key signatures of C, G and F major continue to be used and B♭ major is introduced.

Section 5 is a summary of the low register using all major keys up to two sharps and two flats together with their relative minor keys. The new notes low G♯, throat G♯, C♯ and low F♯ are used and accidentals are encountered more frequently. Time signatures of 2/2 and 3/2 occur for the first time, as do quaver rests.

Section 6 arrives at the clarinet register and remains there! The melodic and rhythmic style is purposely simplified to begin with. Notes from B to upper A are used together with F♯ and C♯ in the key signatures of C, F, G and D major. Some crotchet syncopations occur.

Section 7 joins the two registers together. Once again, all major and minor keys up to two sharps and two flats are used. The time signature of 7/4 makes an appearance.

To the pupil: Why sight-reading?

When you are faced with a new piece and asked to play it, whether at home, in a lesson or in an exam or audition, there is no one there to help you – except yourself! Sight-reading tests your ability to read the time and notes correctly and to observe the phrasing and dynamics quickly.

The aim of this book is to help you teach yourself. The book gives guidance on what to look for and how best to prepare in a very short time by observing the time and key signatures, the shape of the melody and the marks of expression. These short pieces progress gradually to help you build up your confidence and observation and enable you to sight-read accurately. At the end of each section there are three duets to play with your teacher or friends and three pieces with piano accompaniment which will test your ability to sight-read while something else is going on. This is a necessary skill when playing in a band, orchestra or other ensemble.

If you sight-read something every time you play your clarinet you will be amazed how much better you will become. Remember, if you can sight-read most of the tunes you are asked to learn you will be able to concentrate on the 'tricky bits' and complete them quickly.

Think of the tunes in this book as 'mini-pieces' and try to learn them quickly and correctly. Then when you are faced with real sight-reading you will be well-equipped to succeed on a first attempt.

You are on your own now!

Préface

Le propos de ce recueil de déchiffrage pour la clarinette est de fournir une première initiation et un entraînement solide aux principes de la lecture à vue.

Le déchiffrage imposé comme un « travail » ne présente pas grand intérêt s'il n'est supervisé par le maître. L'idéal serait que le déchiffrage prenne régulièrement place dans la routine de travail de l'élève à chaque fois qu'il prend sa clarinette.

L'objectif est ici d'établir l'habitude de la lecture à vue très tôt dans l'étude de la clarinette. Le déchiffrage suppose, bien sûr, que les noms et les valeurs de notes soient complètement assimilés et compris mais il s'appuie également sur la reconnaissance des contours et de la direction.

Ce volume comporte sept sections correspondant à l'introduction progressive de notes, de rythmes, de phrasés, de nuances et de termes italiens nouveaux selon la progression logique rencontrée dans une méthode de clarinette pour débutant. La démarche consiste à fournir des airs et des structures idiomatiques propres à la clarinette de préférence à de stériles exercices de déchiffrage.
Chaque section se termine par trois duos à jouer entre élèves et trois solos accompagnés qui résument les notions qui y ont été abordées.

La section 1 se concentre sur les notes de main gauche de *do* à *la* associées à des rythmes et des indications de mesures simples. Le mouvement mélodique insiste sur la progression par degrés, les structures de phrases simples, les notes répétées et la répétition de motifs mélodiques (séquences).

La section 2 introduit les notes de main droite de *si* à *sol*, les liaisons et des motifs mélodiques légèrement plus arpégés.

La section 3 étend le registre inférieur jusqu'au *fa* ♯ de gorge, *si* ♭ grave, *si* ♭ de gorge, *fa* grave et *mi* grave. Les croches et les noires pointées figurent ici pour la première fois ainsi que l'indication de mesure 5/4 et quelques changements de mesure faciles. Les armures des tonalités de *do* majeur, *sol* majeur et *fa* majeur sont introduites avec des termes italiens et des nuances.

La section 4 présente les mesures composées souvent négligées à 6/8, 9/8 et 12/8 tout en évitant les silences et les liaisons complexes. La tessiture descend jusqu'au *mi* ♭ grave et les altérations accidentelles sont en nombre limité. La tonalité de *si* ♭ majeur s'ajoute à celles de *do* majeur, *sol* majeur et *fa* majeur.

La section 5 est un résumé du jeu dans le registre inférieur dans toutes les tonalités majeures comportant jusqu'à deux dièses ou deux bémols à la clef et leur relatives mineures. Les nouvelles notes *sol* ♯ grave, *sol* ♯ de gorge, *do* ♯ grave et *fa* ♯ grave s'ajoutent et les altérations accidentelles sont plus fréquentes. Les indications de mesures à 2/2 et à 3/2 ainsi que les demi-soupirs y apparaissent pour la première fois.

La section 6 atteint le registre de clairon et y reste ! Le style mélodique et rythmique est volontairement simplifié dans les débuts. Les notes du *si* au *la* aigu sont utilisées ainsi que le *fa* ♯ et le *do* ♯ dans les tonalités de *do* majeur, *fa* majeur, *sol* majeur et *ré* majeur. Quelques noires syncopées y paraissent également.

La section 7 relie les deux registres. Toutes les tonalités dont l'armure comporte jusqu'à deux dièses ou deux bémols y figurent, ainsi que l'indication de mesure à 7/4.

A l'élève : Pourquoi le déchiffrage ?

Lorsque vous vous trouvez face à un nouveau morceau que l'on vous demande de jouer, que ce soit chez vous, pendant une leçon, pour accompagner un autre instrumentiste ou lors d'un examen ou d'une audition, personne d'autre ne peut vous aider que vous-même ! Le déchiffrage met à l'épreuve votre capacité à lire correctement les rythmes et les notes et à observer rapidement le phrasé et les nuances. Ce recueil se propose de vous aider à vous entraîner vous-même. Il vous oriente sur ce que vous devez repérer et sur la meilleure manière de vous préparer en un laps de temps très court en sachant observer les indications de mesure et l'armure de la clef, les contours de la mélodie et les indications expressives. Ces pièces brèves, en progressant par étapes, vous feront prendre de l'assurance, aiguiseront vos observations et vous permettront de lire à vue avec exactitude et aisance. A la fin de chaque section figurent trois duos que vous pourrez jouer avec votre professeur ou des amis et des morceaux avec accompagnement de piano qui vous apprendront à déchiffrer pendant que se déroule une autre partie. Cette capacité est indispensable pour jouer dans un groupe, un orchestre ou un ensemble.

Vous serez stupéfait de vos progrès si vous déchiffrez une pièce à chaque fois que vous vous mettez à la clarinette. N'oubliez pas que si vous êtes capable de lire à vue la plupart des morceaux que vous allez étudier, vous pourrez vous concentrer sur les passages difficiles et les assimiler plus vite.

Considérez ces pages comme des « mini-morceaux » et essayez de les apprendre rapidement et sans erreur de manière à ce que, devant un véritable déchiffrage, vous soyez bien armé pour réussir dès la première lecture.

Vous êtes désormais seul !

Vorwort

Vom–Blatt-Spiel auf der Klarinette 1 möchte zu einer guten Übetechnik verhelfen und frühzeitig für die Einführung der grundlegenden Fähigkeit des Blatt-Spiels sorgen.

Vom-Blatt-Spiel als Hausaufgabe aufzugeben hat wenig Sinn, wenn das Ergebnis nicht vom Lehrer überprüft wird. Idealerweise sollte das Vom-Blatt-Spiel in irgendeiner Form jedes Mal, wenn die Klarinette ausgepackt wird, ein regelmäßiger Bestandteil des Übens werden.

Ziel dieses Buches ist es, bereits von Anfang an diese Gewohnheit im Klarinettenspiel des Schülers zu verankern. Natürlich muss man die Notennamen und Notenwerte komplett kennen und verstanden haben, aber durch das Bewusstsein für Form und Richtung wird das Vom-Blatt-Spiel gleichermaßen unterstützt.

Das Buch hat sieben Teile, die nach und nach neue Noten, Rhythmen, Artikulation, Dynamik und italienische Begriffe in einer logischen Abfolge einführen – ganz ähnlich, wie man es in einer Klarinettenschule für Anfänger auch finden würde. Der Schwerpunkt liegt auf dem Bereitstellen passender Melodien und Strukturen anstelle von sterilen Vom-Blatt-Spiel Übungen. Jeder Teil endet mit drei Schülerduetten und drei begleiteten Stücken, die eine Zusammenfassung des während des jeweiligen Teils vorgestellten Materials darstellen sollen.

Teil 1 beschäftigt sich mit den Tönen c' – a' der linken Hand sowie mit einfachen Rhythmen und Taktarten. Das melodische Material beschäftigt sich mit schrittweiser Bewegung, einfach strukturierten Phrasen sowie sich wiederholenden Noten und melodischen Formen (Sequenzen).

Teil 2 hat bereits einen Notenumfang vom kleinen g – a', Bindungen sowie melodische Formen, die schon etwas stärker gebrochen sind.

Teil 3 erweitert den Tonraum des tiefen Registers um fis', das kleine b, b' sowie das kleine f und e. Achtel- und punktierte Viertelnoten tauchen zum ersten Mal zusammen auf, ebenso die Taktart 5/4 und einige leichte Taktänderungen. Außerdem werden die Tonarten C-, G- und F-Dur eingeführt sowie italienische Bezeichnungen und Dynamikzeichen.

Teil 4 beschäftigt sich mit den oftmals vernachlässigten zusammengesetzten Taktarten 6/8, 9/8 und 12/8, wobei unangenehme Pausen und Bindungen vermieden werden. Das es im tiefen Register wird eingeführt und es gibt eine begrenzte Anzahl von Vorzeichen. Die Tonarten C-, G- und F-Dur stehen weiterhin im Vordergrund, und B-Dur kommt hinzu.

Teil 5 ist eine Zusammenfassung des tiefen Registers. Es werden alle Durtonarten bis zu zwei Kreuz- und B-Vorzeichen sowie ihre verwandten Molltonarten benutzt. Als neue Töne kommen das kleine gis, gis', cis' und das kleine fis hinzu, Vorzeichen gibt es jetzt häufiger. Die Taktarten 2/2 und 3/2 sowie Achtelpausen erscheinen zum ersten Mal.

Teil 6 kommt beim Klarinettenregister an und bleibt auch dort! Für den Anfang sind die Melodik und Rhythmik absichtlich vereinfacht. Es werden die Noten h' – a" zusammen mit fis' und cis" in den Tonarten C-, F-, G- und D-Dur benutzt. Ab und zu taucht eine Synkope aus Viertel- und Achtelnoten auf.

Teil 7 verbindet die beiden Register miteinander. Es werden noch einmal alle Dur- und Moll- Tonarten bis zu zwei Kreuz- und B- Vorzeichen benutzt. Außerdem kommt die Taktart 7/4 vor.

An den Schüler: Warum Vom-Blatt-Spiel?

Wenn du dich einem neuen Musikstück gegenüber siehst und gebeten wirst, es zu spielen, egal, ob zu Hause, im Unterricht, in einem Examen oder einem Vorspiel, gibt es niemanden, der dir helfen kann – nur du selbst! Das Blatt-Spiel testet deine Fähigkeit, Taktarten und Noten richtig zu lesen, sowie Phrasierungen und Dynamik schnell zu erfassen.

Ziel dieses Buches ist es, dir beim Selbstunterricht behilflich zu sein. Das Buch zeigt dir, worauf du achten sollst und wie du dich in sehr kurzer Zeit am besten vorbereitest. Das tust du, indem du dir die jeweilige Takt- und Tonart sowie den Verlauf der Melodie und die Ausdruckszeichen genau anschaust. Die kurzen Musikstücke steigern sich nur allmählich, um sowohl dein Vertrauen und deine Beobachtungsgabe aufzubauen als auch, um dich dazu zu befähigen, exakt vom Blatt zu spielen. Am Ende jeden Teils stehen drei Duette, die du mit deinem Lehrer oder deinen Freunden spielen kannst. Außerdem gibt es drei Stücke mit Klavierbegleitung, die deine Fähigkeit im Blatt-Spiel überprüfen, während gleichzeitig etwas anderes abläuft. Das ist eine wesentliche Fähigkeit, wenn man mit einer Band, einem Orchester oder einer anderen Musikgruppe zusammenspielt.

Wenn du jedes Mal, wenn du Klarinette spielst, auch etwas vom Blatt spielst, wirst du überrascht sein, wie sehr du dich verbesserst. Denke daran: wenn du die meisten Melodien, die du spielen sollst, vom Blatt spielen kannst, kannst du dich auf die ‚schwierigen Teile' konzentrieren und diese viel schneller beherrschen.

Stelle dir die Melodien in diesem Buch als ‚Ministücke' vor und versuche, sie schnell und korrekt zu lernen. Wenn du dann wirklich vom Blatt spielen musst, wirst du bestens ausgerüstet sein, um gleich beim ersten Versuch erfolgreich zu sein.

Jetzt bist du auf dich selbst gestellt!

Section 1 – The left hand
Section 1 – La main gauche
Teil 1 – Die linke Hand

Three steps to success

1. **Look at the top number of the time signature.** It shows the number of beats in a bar. Tap (clap, sing or play on one note) the *rhythm,* feeling the pulse throughout. Count at least one bar of the time signature in your head to set up the pulse before you tap or play each tune.

2. **Look for patterns.** While tapping the rhythm, look at the melodic shape and notice movement by step, skips, repeated notes and sequences (a short, repeated melodic phrase which often rises or falls by step).

3. **Keep going.** Remember, a wrong note or rhythm can be corrected the next time you play it. If you stop, you have doubled the mistake!

Trois étapes vers la réussite

1. **Observez le chiffre supérieur de l'indication de mesure.** Il indique le nombre de pulsations contenues par mesure. Frappez (dans les mains, chantez ou jouez sur une seule note) le *rythme* tout en maintenant une pulsation intérieure constante. Comptez mentalement au moins une mesure complète pour installer la pulsation avant de frapper ou de jouer chaque pièce.

2. **Repérez les motifs.** Tout en frappant le rythme, observez les contours de la mélodie et relevez les mouvements par degrés, les sauts d'intervalles, les notes répétées et les séquences (courtes phrases mélodiques répétées progressant généralement par degrés ascendants ou descendants).

3. **Ne vous arrêtez pas.** Vous corrigerez une fausse note ou un rythme inexact la prochaine fois que vous jouerez. Si vous vous interrompez, vous doublez la faute !

Drei Schritte zum Erfolg

1. **Schaue dir die obere Zahl der Taktangabe an.** Diese zeigt die Anzahl der Schläge in einem Takt. Schlage (klatsche, singe oder spiele auf einer Note) den *Rhythmus*, wobei du immer das Metrum spürst. Zähle mindestens einen Takt lang die Taktangabe im Kopf, um das Metrum zu verinnerlichen, bevor du jede der Melodien klopfst oder spielst.

2. **Achte auf Muster.** Schaue dir die melodische Form an, während du den Rhythmus schlägst und achte auf Bewegungen in Schritten oder Sprüngen, sich wiederholende Noten und Sequenzen (eine kurze, sich wiederholende melodische Phrase, die oft schrittweise ansteigt oder abfällt).

3. **Bleibe dran.** Denke daran: eine falsche Note oder ein falscher Rhythmus kann beim nächsten Mal korrigiert werden. Wenn du aber aufhörst zu spielen, verdoppelst du den Fehler!

8

Section 1 – The left hand
Section 1 – La main gauche
Teil 1 – Die linke Hand

Play at a steady speed and with a bold tone. Notice the melodic shapes.

Jouez à une vitesse régulière et avec une sonorité ferme. Repérez les motifs mélodiques.

Spiele in einem gleichmäßigen Tempo und mit einem kräftigen Ton. Achte auf die melodischen Figuren.

Notes C – E

Notes *do* à *mi*

Die Noten c' – e'

1.

2.

3.

4.

5.

6.

Watch out for skips.

Attention aux sauts d'intervalles.

Achte auf Sprünge.

7.

Mark melodic shapes and patterns with a pencil.

Notes C – F

Tracez les contours mélodiques et les motifs au crayon.

Notes *do* à *fa*

Kennzeichne melodische Figuren und Muster mit einem Bleistift.

Die Noten c' – g'

Notes C – G

Notes *do* à *sol*

Die Noten c' – g'

16.

Notes C – A   Notes *do* à *la*   Die Noten c' – a'

17.

18.

19.

20.

21.

22.

23.

Steady and positive   Régulier et affirmé   Gleichmäßig und bestimmt

24.

Smooth and flowing   Doux et coulant   Weich und fließend

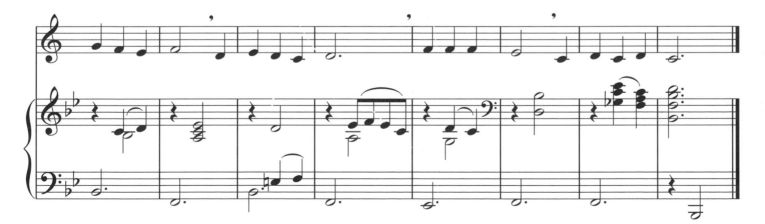

25.

Steady and bold   Régulier et vigoureux   Gleichmäßig und kräftig

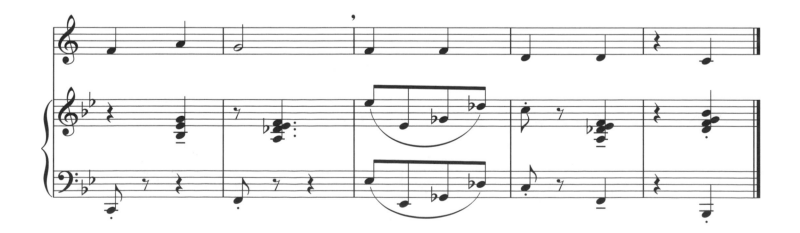

Section 2 – The right hand
Section 2 – La main droite
Teil 2 – Die rechte Hand

Four steps to success

1. **Look at the top number of the time signature.** Tap (clap, sing or play on one note) the *rhythm,* feeling the pulse throughout. Count at least one bar of the time signature in your head to set up the pulse before you tap or play each tune.

2. **Look for patterns.** While tapping the rhythm, look at the melodic shape and notice movement by step, skips, repeated notes and sequences.

3. **Notice the slurring.** Slurring is often very logical. Similar phrases will usually have the same articulation.

4. **Keep going!**

Quatre étapes vers la réussite

1. **Observez le chiffre supérieur de l'indication de mesure.** Frappez (dans les mains, chantez ou jouez sur une seule note) le *rythme* tout en maintenant une pulsation intérieure constante. Comptez mentalement au moins une mesure pour installer la pulsation avant de frappez ou de jouer chaque pièce.

2. **Repérez les motifs.** Tout en frappant le rythme, observez les contours de la mélodie et relevez les mouvements par degrés, les sauts d'intervalles, les notes répétées ou les séquences.

3. **Observez les liaisons de phrasé.** Les liaisons suivent généralement une logique. Les phrases similaires sont habituellement articulées de la même façon.

4. **Ne vous arrêtez pas !**

Vier Schritte zum Erfolg

1. **Schaue dir die obere Zahl der Taktangabe an.** Diese zeigt die Anzahl der Schläge in einem Takt. Schlage (klatsche, singe oder spiele auf einer Note) den *Rhythmus*, wobei du immer das Metrum spürst. Zähle mindestens einen Takt lang die Taktangabe im Kopf, um das Metrum zu verinnerlichen, bevor du jede der Melodien klopfst oder spielst.

2. **Achte auf Muster.** Schaue dir die melodische Form an, während du den Rhythmus schlägst und achte auf Bewegungen in Schritten oder Sprüngen, sich wiederholende Noten und Sequenzen.

3. **Konzentriere dich auf die Bindungen.** Bindungen sind oft sehr logisch. Ähnliche Phrasen haben normalerweise auch dieselbe Artikulation.

4. **Bleibe dran!**

Section 2 – The right hand
Section 2 – La main droite
Teil 2 – Die rechte Hand

Notice the slurs.
New Note B

Repérez les liaisons de phrasé.
Nouvelle note: *si*

Achte auf die Bindungen.
Als neue Note das kleine h

26.

27.

28.

29.

New note A

Nouvelle Note: *la*

Als neue Note das kleine a

30.

31.

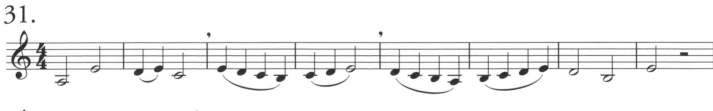

32.

New note G   Nouvelle note: *sol*   Als neue Note das kleine g

33.

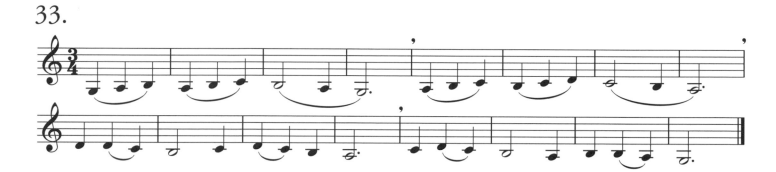

34.

35.

36.

37.

15

38.

39.

40.

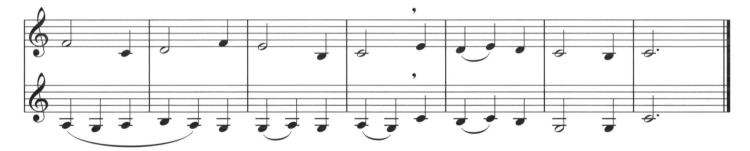

41.

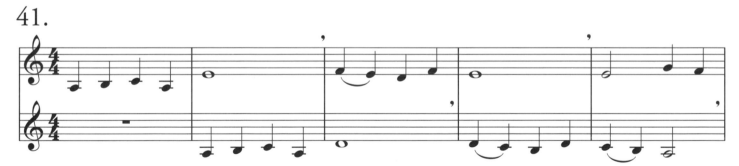

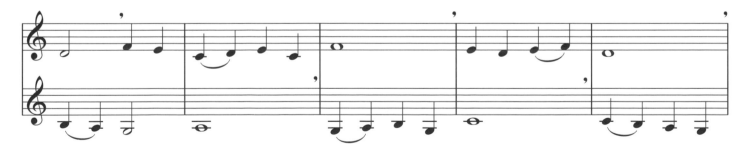

42.

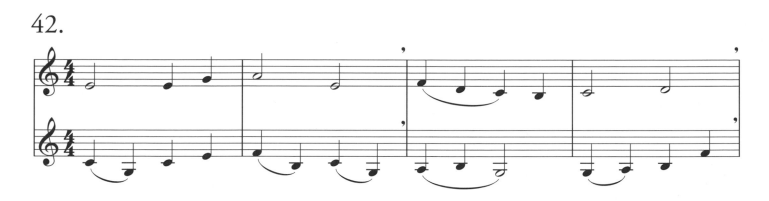

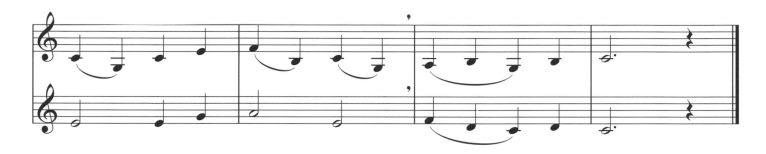

43.

Steady   Régulier   Gleichmäßig

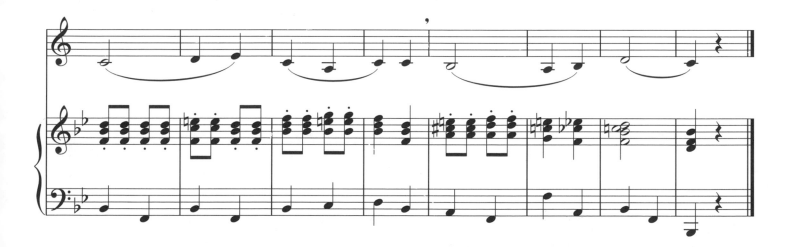

44.

Graceful   Gracieux   Anmutig

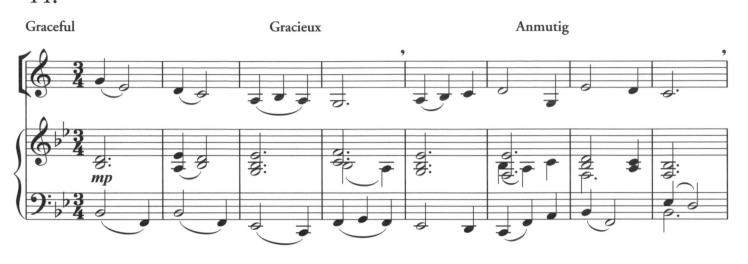

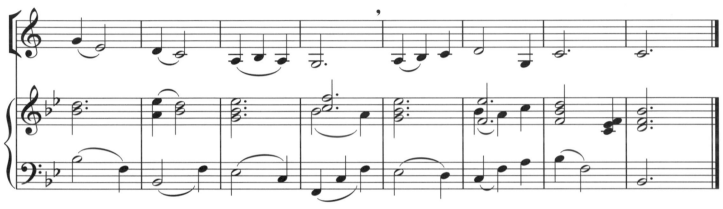

45.

Grooving   Eclatant !   Mit Schwung – fetzig!

Section 3 – More of the low (chalumeau) register
Section 3 – Plus loin dans le registre inférieur (chalumeau)
Teil 3 – Noch mehr aus dem Chalumeau-Register

Five steps to success

1. **Look at the top number of the time signature.** Tap (clap, sing or play on one note) the *rhythm,* feeling the pulse throughout. Count at least one bar of the time signature in your head to set up the pulse before you tap or play each tune.

2. **Look between the treble clef and the time signature for any sharps or flats.** Make sure you know which notes these apply to and notice where they occur in the melody.

3. **Look for patterns.** While tapping the rhythm, look at the melodic shape and notice movement by step, skips, repeated notes and sequences.

4. **Notice the articulation and dynamics.** Slurring is often very logical. Similar phrases will usually have the same articulation. Observe the dynamic shapes and notice if they change suddenly or gradually.

5. **Keep going!**

Performance directions used in Section 3
(You may note all directions and translations on the glossary page at the back of the book)

Adagio – slowly
Allegretto – moderately fast
Allegro – lively
Andante – at a walking pace
Andantino – a little faster than Andante
Animato – animated
Con brio – with life
Con grazia – with grace
Con moto – with movement
Crescendo (*cresc.*) – getting louder
Giocoso – joyful
Legato – smoothly
Maestoso – majestically
Marcato (*marc.*) – marked
Moderato – moderate speed
Poco a poco – little by little
Risoluto – resolute
Ritardando (rit.) – becoming slower
Sostenuto – sustained

Cinq étapes vers la réussite

1. **Observez le chiffre supérieur de l'indication de mesure.** Il indique le nombre de pulsations contenues par mesure. Frappez (dans les mains, chantez ou jouez sur un seule note) le *rythme* tout en maintenant une pulsation intérieure constante. Comptez mentalement au moins une mesure pour installer la pulsation avant de frapper ou de jouer chaque pièce.

2. **Vérifiez les dièses ou les bémols placés entre la clef de *sol* et les chiffres indicateurs de mesure.** Ceux-ci constituent l'armure de la tonalité. Assurez-vous des notes altérées et repérez-les dans la mélodie.

3. **Repérez les motifs.** Tout en frappant le rythme, observez les contours de la mélodie et relevez les déplacements par degrés, les sauts d'intervalles, les notes répétées et les séquences (courte phrase mélodique répétées progressant généralement par degrés ascendants ou descendants).

4. **Observez le phrasé et les nuances.** Les liaisons suivent généralement une logique. Les phrases similaires seront habituellement articulées de la même façon. Notez les nuances dynamiques et leurs changements subits ou progressifs.

5. **Ne vous arrêtez pas !**

Indications d'exécution utilisées dans la section 3
(Vous pourrez noter toutes les indications et leur traduction sur la page de glossaire en fin de volume).

Adagio – lentement
Allegretto – modérément vite
Allegro – rapide
Andante – allant
Andantino – un peu plus allant
Animato – animé
Con brio – avec éclat
Con grazia – avec grâce
Con moto – avec mouvement
Crescendo (*cresc.*) – de plus en plus fort
Giocoso – joyeux
Legato – lié
Maestoso – majestueux
Marcato (*marc.*) – marqué
Moderato – modéré
Poco a poco – peu à peu
Risoluto – résolu
Ritardando (rit.) – progressivement plus lent
Sostenuto – soutenu

Fünf Schritte zum Erfolg

1. **Schaue dir die obere Zahl der Taktangabe an.** Diese zeigt die Anzahl der Schläge in einem Takt. Schlage (klatsche, singe oder spiele auf einer Note) den *Rhythmus*, wobei du immer das Metrum spürst. Zähle mindestens einen Takt lang die Taktangabe im Kopf, um das Metrum zu verinnerlichen, bevor du jede der Melodien klopfst oder spielst.

2. **Achte auf Kreuz- und B-Vorzeichen zwischen dem Notenschlüssel und der Taktangabe.** Überzeuge dich davon, dass du weißt, auf welche Noten sich diese beziehen und finde heraus, wo sie in der Melodie auftauchen.

3. **Achte auf Muster.** Schaue dir die melodische Form an, während du den Rhythmus schlägst und achte auf Bewegungen in Schritten oder Sprüngen, sich wiederholende Noten und Sequenzen.

4. **Beachte Artikulation und Dynamik.** Bindungen sind oft sehr logisch. Ähnliche Phrasen haben normalerweise auch dieselbe Artikulation. Schaue dir die dynamischen Formen genau an und registriere, ob sie sich plötzlich oder allmählich ändern.

5. **Bleibe dran!**

Vortragsangaben, die in Teil 3 verwendet werden:
(Alle Vortragsangaben und ihre Übersetzungen kannst du dir auf der entsprechenden Seite im Glossar notieren)

Adagio – langsam
Allegretto – gemäßigt schnell
Allegro – lebhaft
Andante – gehend
Andantino – ein bisschen schneller als Andante
Animato – angeregt
Con brio – mit Leben
Con grazia – mit Anmut
Con moto – mit Bewegung
Crescendo (*cresc.*) – lauter werdend
Giocoso – scherzhaft
Legato – gebunden
Maestoso – majestätisch
Marcato (*marc.*) – markiert
Moderato – gemäßigt
Poco a poco – nach und nach
Risoluto – entschieden
Ritardando (rit.) – langsamer werdend
Sostenuto – zurückhaltend

Section 3 – More of the low (chalumeau) register
Section 3 – Plus loin dans le registre inférieur (chalumeau)
Teil 3 – Noch mehr aus dem Chalumeau-Register

G major	*Sol* majeur	G-Dur
New note F♯	Nouvelle note: *fa* ♯	Die neue Note fis'

46. Allegretto

47. Allegro

This piece begins on the fourth beat of the bar in 4-time.
Count 1 2 3 before you begin.

Cette pièce débute sur le 4ᵉ temps d'une mesure à 4 temps.

Comptez 1, 2, 3 avant de commencer. Dieses Stück beginnt auf dem vierten Schlag in einem 4/4-Takt. Zähle daher

48. Risoluto

This piece begins on the third beat of the bar in 3-time. Count 1 2 3 1 2 before you begin.

Cette pièce débute sur le 3ᵉ temps d'une mesure à 3 temps. Comptez 1, 2, 3, 1, 2 avant de commencer.

Dieses Stück beginnt auf dem dritten Schlag in einem 3/4-Takt. Zähle daher 1 2 3 1 2 vor, bevor du anfängst.

Andante

F major
New note low B♭

Fa majeur
Nouvelle note: *si* ♭ grave

F-Dur
Das kleine b als neue Note

50.
Con brio

51.
Moderato

New note low F

Nouvelle note *fa* grave

Das klein f als neue Note.

This piece begins on the second beat of a bar in 2-time. Count 1 2 1 before you begin.

Cette pièce débute sur le 2ᵉ temps d'une mesure à 2 temps.
Comptez 1, 2, 1 avant de commencer.

Dieses Stück beginnt auf dem zweiten Schlag eines 2/4-Taktes. Zähle 1 2 1 vor, bevor du anfängst.

52.
Con moto

This piece begins on the third beat of a bar in 3-time. Count 1 2 3 1 2 before you begin.

Cette pièce commence sur le 3ᵉ temps d'une mesure à 3 temps. Comptez 1, 2, 3, 1, 2 avant de commencer.

Dieses Stück beginnt auf dem dritten Schlag in einem 3/4-Takt. Zähle daher 1 2 3 1 2 vor, bevor du anfängst.

53.
Con grazia

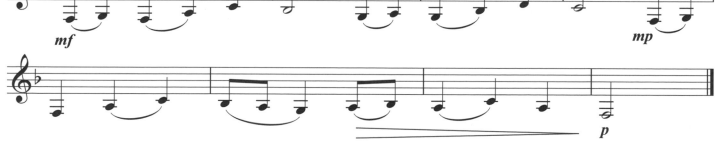

F major
This piece begins on the fourth beat of the bar in 4-time. Count 1 2 3 before you begin.

fa majeur
Cette pièce commence sur le 4ᵉ temps d'une mesure à 4 temps.
Comptez 1, 2, 3 avant de commencer.

F-Dur
Dieses Stück beginnt auf dem vierten Schlag eines 4/4-Taktes. Zähle 1 2 3 vor, bevor du anfängst.

(Pentatonic G, B♭, C, D, F)

(Mode pentatonique: *sol, si ♭, do, ré, fa*)

(Eine Pentatonik mit den Tönen G, B, C, D, F)

New note low E

Nouvelle note: *mi* grave

Das kleine e als neue Note

Count 1 2 3 4 5 before you begin.

Comptez 1, 2, 3, 4, 5 avant de commencer.

Zähle 1 2 3 4 5 vor, bevor du beginnst.

G major
This piece begins on the fifth beat of a bar in 5-time.
Count 1 2 3 4 before you begin.

sol majeur
Cette pièce débute sur le 5ᵉ temps d'une mesure à 5 temps. Comptez 1, 2, 3, 4 avant de commencer.

G-Dur
Dieses Stück beginnt auf dem fünften Schlag eines 5/4-Taktes. Zähle 1 2 3 4 vor, bevor du beginnst.

58.

C major
This piece begins on the fifth beat of a bar in 5-time.
Count 1 2 3 4 before you begin.

do majeur
Cette pièce débute sur le 5ᵉ temps d'une mesure à 5 temps. Comptez 1, 2, 3, 4 avant de commencer.

C-Dur
Dieses Stück beginnt auf dem fünften Schlag eines 5/4-Taktes. Zähle 1 2 3 4 vor, bevor du beginnst.

59.

G major
Look out for the ♩. ♪ rhythms.

sol majeur
Attention aux rythmes ♩. ♪

G-Dur
Achte auf den ♩. ♪ Rhythmus.

60.

Look out for the ♩. ♪ rhythms.

Attention aux rythmes ♩. ♪

Achte auf den ♩. ♪ Rhythmus.

61.

24

G major
Look out for the ♩. ♪ rhythms.

sol majeur
Attention aux rythmes ♩. ♪

G-Dur
Achte auf den ♩. ♪ Rhythmus.

62.

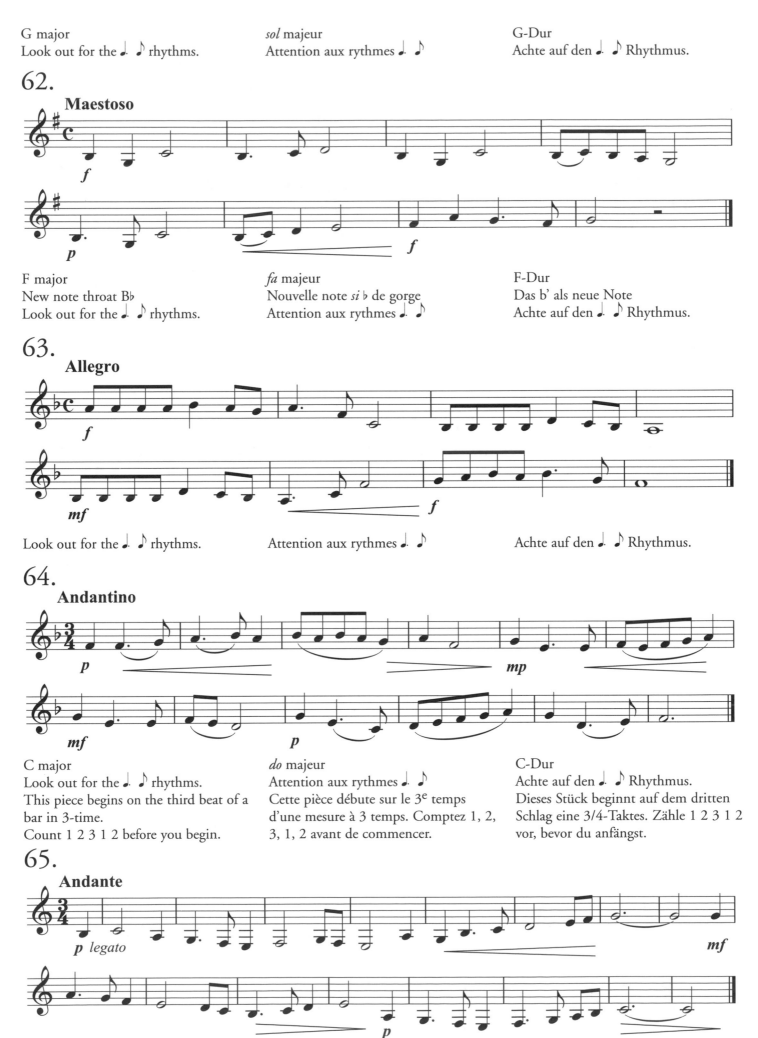

F major
New note throat B♭
Look out for the ♩. ♪ rhythms.

fa majeur
Nouvelle note *si* ♭ de gorge
Attention aux rythmes ♩. ♪

F-Dur
Das b' als neue Note
Achte auf den ♩. ♪ Rhythmus.

63.

Look out for the ♩. ♪ rhythms.

Attention aux rythmes ♩. ♪

Achte auf den ♩. ♪ Rhythmus.

64.

C major
Look out for the ♩. ♪ rhythms.
This piece begins on the third beat of a bar in 3-time.
Count 1 2 3 1 2 before you begin.

do majeur
Attention aux rythmes ♩. ♪
Cette pièce débute sur le 3ᵉ temps d'une mesure à 3 temps. Comptez 1, 2, 3, 1, 2 avant de commencer.

C-Dur
Achte auf den ♩. ♪ Rhythmus.
Dieses Stück beginnt auf dem dritten Schlag eine 3/4-Taktes. Zähle 1 2 3 1 2 vor, bevor du anfängst.

65.

C major   *do* majeur   C-Dur

66.

Con brio

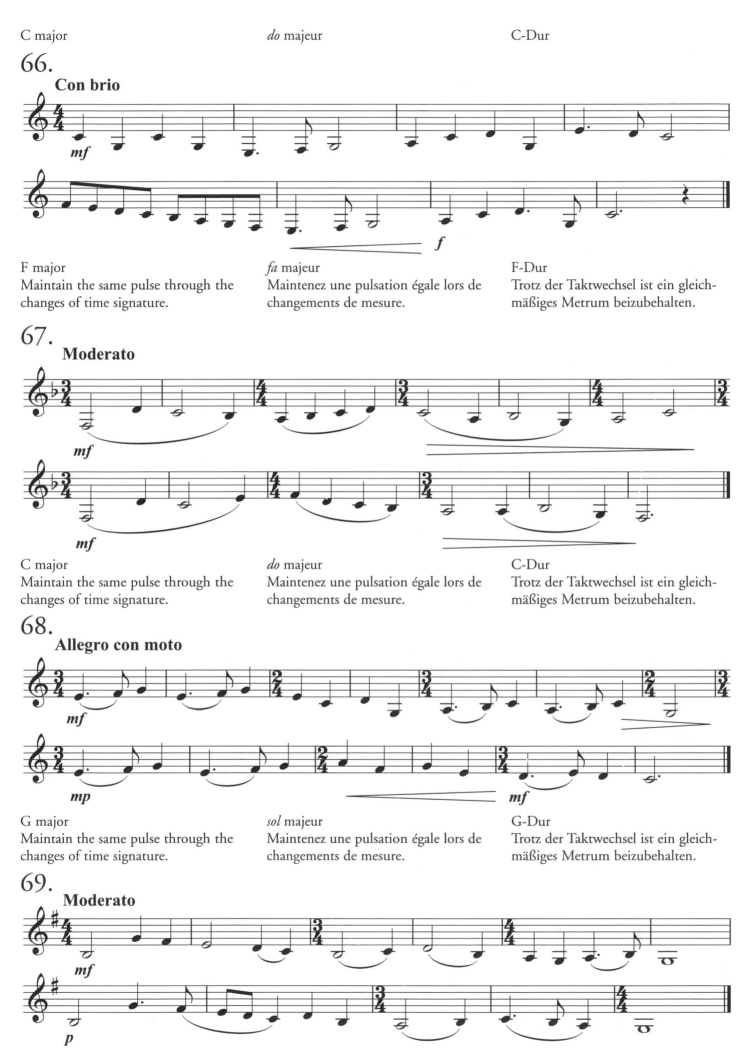

F major   *fa* majeur   F-Dur
Maintain the same pulse through the   Maintenez une pulsation égale lors de   Trotz der Taktwechsel ist ein gleich-
changes of time signature.   changements de mesure.   mäßiges Metrum beizubehalten.

67.

Moderato

C major   *do* majeur   C-Dur
Maintain the same pulse through the   Maintenez une pulsation égale lors de   Trotz der Taktwechsel ist ein gleich-
changes of time signature.   changements de mesure.   mäßiges Metrum beizubehalten.

68.

Allegro con moto

G major   *sol* majeur   G-Dur
Maintain the same pulse through the   Maintenez une pulsation égale lors de   Trotz der Taktwechsel ist ein gleich-
changes of time signature.   changements de mesure.   mäßiges Metrum beizubehalten.

69.

Moderato

70.

Con moto

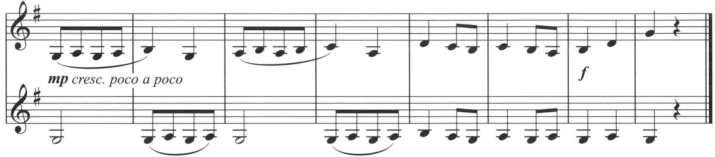

71.

Allegretto

72. **Marcato**

73.

Giocoso

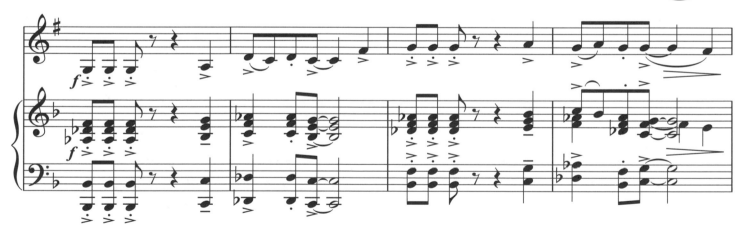

74.

Animato

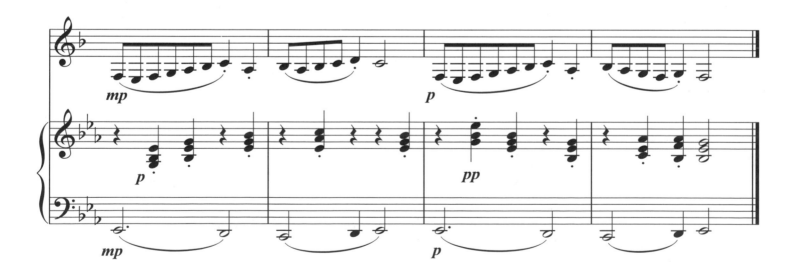

75.

Jazz waltz   Valse jazz   Jazz Waltzer

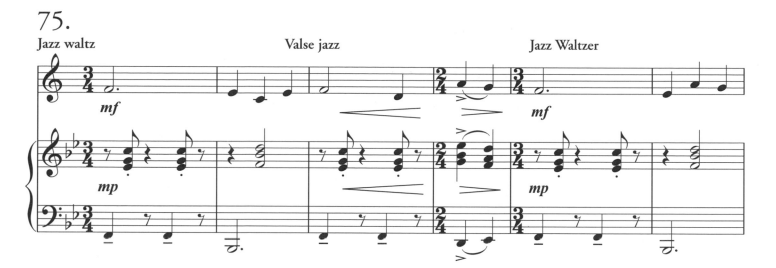

Section 4 – Compound time signatures
Section 4 – Mesures composées
Teil 4 – Zusammengesetzte Taktarten

Key steps to understanding compound rhythms

1. The time signatures of 6/8, 9/8 and 12/8 are known as compound time signatures. Each beat is divides into three equal parts (say the word 'pineapple' to a beat) unlike simple time signatures (4/4) which divide into 2 (say the word 'mango' to a beat).

2. The most common of these compound time signatures is 6/8 and means there are 6 quavers (1/8 notes) in a bar. In 6/8 there are two groups of three quavers so each bar will be counted in 2.

pine - ap - ple pine - ap - ple

3. The opening two bars of 'Humpty Dumpty' contain three of the most common rhythms in compound time signatures.

Hump - ty Dump - ty sat on the wall.

4. In all compound time signatures in this section 𝅗𝅥. = 2 beats, 𝅘𝅥. = 1 beat, 𝅘𝅥 = 2/3 of a beat and 𝅘𝅥𝅮 = 1/3 of a beat.

5.
6/8 is 2 beats in a bar
(two groups of three quavers).
9/8 is 3 beats in a bar
(three groups of three quavers).
12/8 is 4 beats in a bar
(four groups of three quavers).

Additional performance directions used in Section 4
(Note these on the glossary page at the back of the book)

Alla marcia – in the style of a March
Con spirito – with spirit
Espressivo *(espress.)* – expressively
Pastorale – in a pastoral style
Pesante – heavily
Rallantando (rall.) – becoming slower
Vivace – fast and lively
Vivo – lively

Etapes essentielles à la compréhension des mesures composées

1. 3/8, 6/8, 9/8 et 12/8 constituent les indications de mesures composées. Chaque temps y est divisé en trois parties égales (prononcez le mot « éléphant » sur chaque temps) à la différence des mesures simples (2/4, 3/4, et 4/4) dont les temps se divisent en deux parties égales (prononcez le mot « canard » sur chaque temps).

2. 6/8 est l'indication de mesure composée la plus fréquente et signifie que chaque mesure contient six croches égales. Chaque mesure à 6/8 contient deux groupes de trois croches. C'est donc une mesure à deux temps.

é - lé - phant é - lé - phant

3. Les deux premières mesures de *Humpty Dumpty* présentent les trois rythmes les plus fréquemment rencontrés dans les mesures composées

Hump - ty Dump - ty sat on the wall.

4. Dans toutes les mesures composées de cette section 𝅗𝅥. = deux temps, 𝅘𝅥. = un temps, 𝅘𝅥 = deux tiers de temps, 𝅘𝅥𝅮 = un tiers de temps

5.
6/8 indique deux temps par mesure
(deux groupes de trois croches)
9/8 indique trois temps par mesure
(trois groupes de trois croches)
12/8 indique quatre temps par mesure
(quatre groupes de trois croches)

Indications d'exécution supplémentaires rencontrées dans la section 4
(à inscrire sur la page de glossaire en fin de volume)

Alla marcia – en style de marche
Con spirito – avec esprit
Espressivo *(espress.)* – expressif
Pastorale – en style de pastorale
Pesante – pesamment
Rallantando (rall.) – en ralentissant
Vivace – rapidement
Vivo – vif

Die entscheidenden Schritte, um zusammengesetzte Rhythmen zu verstehen

1. Die Taktarten 3/8, 6/8, 9/8 und 12/8 sind als zusammengesetzte Taktarten bekannt. Jeder Schlag ist in drei gleichlange Teile aufgeteilt (sage das Wort ‚*Murmeltier*' auf einen Schlag) im Gegensatz zu einfachen Taktarten (4/4), die in zwei gleichlange Teile aufgeteilt sind (sage das Wort ‚*Mango*' auf einen Schlag).

2. Von diesen Taktarten kommt der 6/8-Takt am häufigsten vor. Er besteht aus sechs gleichlangen Achteln pro Takt. Im 6/8- Takt gibt es zwei Gruppen mit je drei Achtelnoten. Jeder Takt hat also zwei Schläge.

Mur - mel - tier Mur - mel - tier

3. Die zwei Eröffnungstakte des Kinderliedes *Humpty Dumpty* beinhalten drei der häufigsten Rhythmen, die in zusammengesetzten Taktarten vorkommen.

Hump - ty Dump - ty sat on the wall.

4. In allen zusammengesetzten Taktarten in diesem Abschnitt sind 𝅗𝅥. = zwei Schläge, 𝅘𝅥. = ein Schlag, 𝅘𝅥 = 2/3 eines Schlages und 𝅘𝅥𝅮 = 1/3 eines Schlages

5.
Der **6/8-Takt** hat 2 Schläge pro Takt
(zwei Gruppen mit drei Achteln)
Der **9/8-Takt** hat 3 Schläge pro Takt
(drei Gruppen mit drei Achteln)
Der **12/8-Takt** hat 4 Schläge pro Takt
(vier Gruppen mit drei Achteln)

Zusätzliche Vortragsangaben, die in Teil 4 vorkommen:
(Alle Vortragsangaben und ihre Übersetzungen kannst du dir auf der entsprechenden Seite im Glossar notieren)

Alla marcia – im Marschstil
Con spirito – mit Geist
Espressivo (espress.) – ausdrucksvoll
Pastorale – im ländlichen Stil
Pesante – schwer
Rallantando (rall.) – langsamer werdend
Vivace – schnell und lebhaft
Vivo – mit Lebhaftigkeit

Section 4 – Compound time signatures
Section 4 – Mesures composées
Teil 4 – Zusammengesetzte Taktarten

C major
Count 1 (2 3) 2 (2 3) before you begin. Subdivide each beat into three smaller beats.

do majeur
Comptez 1 (2 3) 2 (2 3) avant de commencer. Divisez chaque temps en trois subdivisions

C-Dur
Zähle 1 (2 3) 2 (2 3), bevor du anfängst. Unterteile jeden Schlag in drei kürzere Schläge.

76.

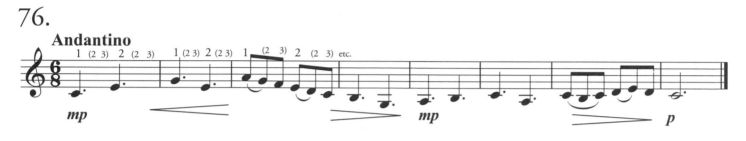

G major
Count 1 2 before you begin.

sol majeur
Comptez 1, 2 avant de commencer.

G-Dur
Zähle 1 2 bevor du anfängst.

77.

F major
Count 1 2 before you begin.

fa majeur
Comptez 1, 2 avant de commencer.

F-Dur
Zähle 1 2 bevor du anfängst.

78.

F major
Count 1 2 3 before you begin.

fa majeur
Comptez 1, 2, 3 avant de commencer.

F-Dur
Zähle 1 2 3, bevor du anfängst.

79.

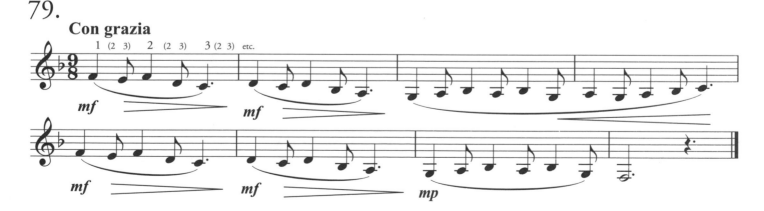

G major	*sol* majeur	G-Dur
Count 1 2 3 before you begin.	Comptez 1, 2, 3 avant de commencer.	Zähle 1 2 3 bevor du anfängst.

80.

Allegretto

C major	*do* majeur	C-Dur
Watch out for F♯ accidentals	Attention au *fa* ♯ accidentelles.	Achte auf das fis-Vorzeichen.
Count 1 2 3 before you begin.	Comptez 1, 2, 3 avant de commencer.	Zähle 1 2 3 bevor du anfängst.

81.

Allegretto

Watch out for accidentals.	Attention au alterations accidentelles.	Achte auf etwaige Vorzeichen.
Count 1 2 3 4 before you begin.	Comptez 1, 2, 3, 4 avant de commencer.	Zähle 1 2 3 4 bevor du anfängst.

82. **Allegro**

Bb major.
New note Eb.
Count 1 2 3 4 before you begin.

si b majeur.
Nouvelle note *mi* b.
Count 1, 2, 3, 4 avant de commencer..

B-Dur
Neue Note es'.
Zähle 1 2 3 4 bevor du anfängst.

83.
Moderato

Count 1 (2 3) 1 (2 3) before you begin.

Comptez 1 (2, 3), 1 (2, 3) avant de commencer.

Zähle 1 (2 3) 1 (2 3) bevor du anfängst.

84.*
Con spirito

C major
Watch out for accidentals.
Count 1 (2 3) 1 (2 3) before you begin.

do majeur
Attentions aux altérations accidentelles.
Comptez 1 (2, 3), 1 (2, 3) avant de commencer.

C-Dur
Achte auf etwaige Vorzeichen.
Zähle 1 (2 3) 1 (2 3) bevor du anfängst.

85.
Vivace

* Although strictly simple time, 3/8 often takes on the characteristic of a compound time signature. It was therefore decided to include 3/8 pieces in this section.

34

86.

Moderato

mf

p

mf

87.

Pastorale

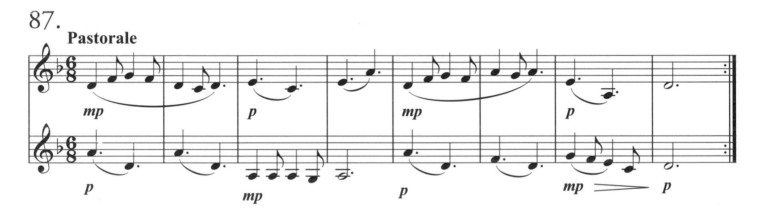

mp *p* *mp* *p*

p *mp* *p* *mp* *p*

88.

Pesante

f *p* *mp*

f *mp* *f*

89.

90.

Alla marcia

91.
Vivo

Section 5 – Completing the chalumeau register
Sectio 5 – Le registre de chalumeau en entier
Teil 5 – Das Vervollständigen des Chalumeau-Registers

Six steps to success

1. **Look at the time signature.** Tap (clap, sing or play on one note) the *rhythm,* feeling the pulse throughout. Count at least one bar of the time signature in your head to set up the pulse before you tap or play each tune.

2. **Look between the treble clef and the time signature for any sharps or flats.** Make sure you know which notes these apply to and notice where they occur in the melody. Sort out the fingerings before you begin.

3. **Look out for accidentals.** Check that you know the fingering before you arrive at the note.

4. **Look for patterns.** While tapping the rhythm, look at the melodic shape and notice movement by step, skips, repeated notes and sequences.

5. **Notice the articulation and dynamics.**

6. **Keep going!**

Two new time signatures
2/2 Two minim (half note) beats per bar (a minim = 1 beat)
3/2 Three minim (half note) beats per bar (a minim = 1 beat)

Performance directions used in Section 5
(Note these on the glossary page at the back of the book)

Con amore – lovingly
Diminuendo *(dim.)* – gradually softer
Lento – slowly
Ma non troppo – but not too much
Meno mosso – slower
Molto – a lot
Mysterioso – mysteriously
Presto – very fast
Sonore – sonorous
Veloce – swiftly
Vigoroso – vigorous

Six étapes vers la réussite

1. **Observez l'indication de mesure.** Frappez (dans les mains, chantez ou jouez sur une seule note) le rythme tout en maintenant une pulsation intérieure constante. Comptez mentalement au moins une mesure pour installer la pulsation avant de frapper le rythme ou de jouer la pièce.

2. **Vérifiez les dièses ou les bémols placés entre la clef de *sol* et l'indication de mesure.** Ils constituent l'armure de la tonalité. Assurez vous des notes altérées et repérez-les dans la mélodie. Pensez aux doigtés avant de commencer.

3. **Recherchez les altérations accidentelles.** Contrôlez votre doigté avant d'atteindre la note.

4. **Repérez les motifs.** Tout en frappant le rythme, observez les contours de la mélodie et relevez les mouvements par degré, les sauts d'intervalles, les notes répétées et les séquences.

5. **Observez le phrasé et les nuances.**

6. **Ne vous arrêtez pas !**

Deux nouvelles indications de mesure
2/2 : deux blanche par mesure (blanche = 1 temps)
3/2 : trois blanches par mesure (blanche = 1 temps)

Indications d'exécution utilisées dans cette section
(à inscrire sur la page de glossaire en fin de volume)
Con amore – avec tendresse
Diminuendo *(dim.)* – de plus en plus doux
Lento – lent
Ma non troppo – mais pas trop
Meno mosso – plus lent
Molto – beaucoup
Mysterioso – mystérieux
Presto – très rapide
Sonore – sonore
Veloce – rapide
Vigoroso – vigoureux

Sechs Schritte zum Erfolg

1. **Schaue dir die Taktangabe an.** Schlage (klatsche, singe oder spiele auf einer Note) den *Rhythmus*, wobei du immer das Metrum spürst. Zähle mindestens einen Takt lang die Takt-angabe im Kopf, um das Metrum zu verinnerlichen, bevor du jede der Melodien klopfst oder spielst.

2. **Achte auf Kreuz- und B- Vorzeichen zwischen dem Notenschlüssel und der Taktangabe.** Versichere dich, dass du weißt, auf welche Noten sich diese be-ziehen und finde heraus, wo in der Melodie sie auftauchen. Überprüfe ihre Griffweise, bevor du zu spielen anfängst.

3. **Suche nach Notenvorzeichen.** Stelle sicher, dass du die Griffweise kennst, bevor du diese Note erreichst.

4. **Achte auf Muster.** Schaue dir die melodische Form an, während du den Rhythmus schlägst und achte auf Bewegungen in Schritten oder Sprüngen, sich wiederholende Noten und Sequenzen.

5. **Beachte Artikulation und Dynamik.**

6. **Bleibe dran!**

Zwei neue Taktarten
Der 2/2- Takt hat zwei Schläge pro Takt (eine halbe Note = 1 Schlag)
Der 3/2- Takt hat drei Schläge pro Takt (eine halbe Note = 1 Schlag)

Vortragsangaben für den Teil 5
(Notiere diese auf der entsprechenden Seite im Glossar)

Con amore – liebevoll
Diminuendo *(dim.)* – allmählich leiser
Lento – langsam
Ma non troppo – aber nicht zu viel
Meno mosso – langsamer
Molto – viel
Mysterioso – geheimnisvoll
Presto – sehr schnell
Sonore – klangvoll
Veloce – geschwind
Vigoroso – kraftvoll

Section 5 – Completing the chalumeau register

Sectio 5 – Le registre de chalumeau en entier

Teil 5 – Das Vervollständigen des Chalumeau-Registers

| C major | *do* majeur | C-Dur |

92.

March

A minor (relative minor of C major)
New Notes throat G♯ and low G♯.

la mineur (relative de *do* majeur)
Nouvelles notes: *sol* ♯ et *sol* ♯ grave.

A-Moll (die Paralleltonart von C-Dur)
Die neue Noten sind das gis' und das kleine gis.

93.

Lento e espressivo

94.

Veloce

F major   *fa* majeur   F-Dur

95. Presto

D minor (relative minor of F major)   *ré* mineur (relative mineur de *fa*   D-Moll (die Paralleltonart von F-Dur)
New note C♯   majeur). Nouvelle note *do* ♯   Als neue Note das cis'

96. Andantino

97. Moderato

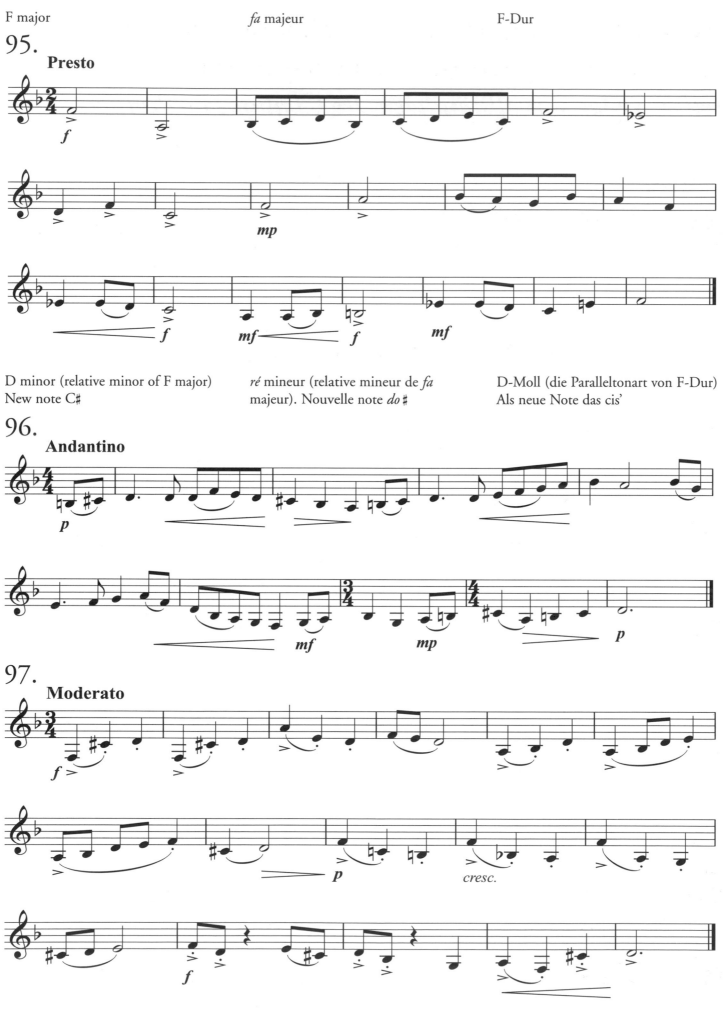

Bb major   Sib majeur   B-Dur

98.

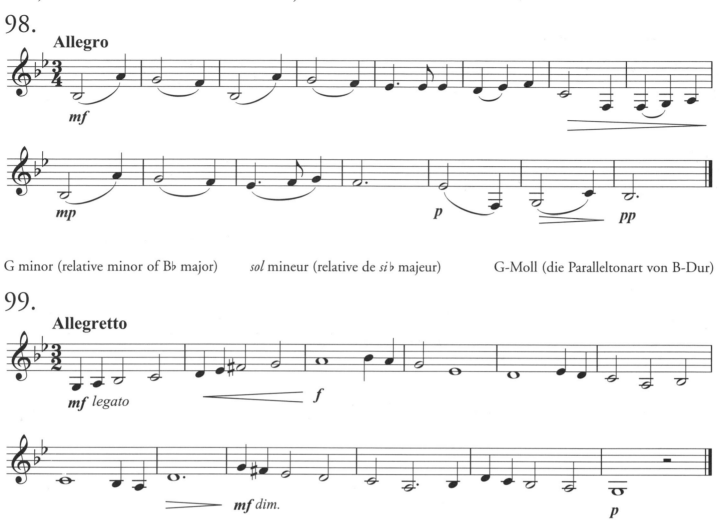

G minor (relative minor of Bb major)   sol mineur (relative de sib majeur)   G-Moll (die Paralleltonart von B-Dur)

99.

100.

101.

42

D major   *ré* majeur   D-Dur

New note low F♯   Nouvelle note: *fa* ♯ grave   Als neue Note das kleine fis

B minor (relative minor of D major)   *si* mineur (relative mineure   H-Moll (die Paralleltonart zu D-Dur)
                                     de *ré* majeur)

G major   *sol* majeur   G-Dur

106.

Marcato

E minor (relative minor of G major)   *mi* mineur (relative mineure de *sol* majeur)   E-Moll (die Paralleltonart von G-Dur)

107.

Allegretto

108.

Moderate blues – with a beat!

44

109.
Vigoroso

110.
Lilting

111.
Waltz

112.

Moderato e pesante

113.

Con amore

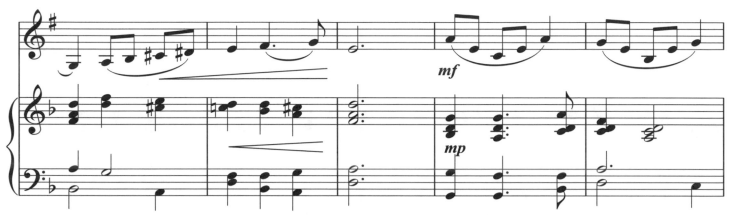

poco meno mosso　　　　　　　　　　　　**molto rall.**

114.

Animato

Section 6 – The upper (clarinet) register
Section 6 – Le registre supérieur (clairon)
Teil 6 – Das obere (Klarinetten-) Register

From now on you will need to decide the key signature for yourself.

Six steps to success

1. **Look at the time signature.** Tap (clap, sing or play on one note) the *rhythm,* feeling the pulse throughout. Count at least one bar of the time signature in your head to set up the pulse before you tap or play each tune.

2. **Look between the treble clef and the time signature for any sharps or flats.** Make sure you know which notes these apply to and notice where they occur in the melody. Sort out the fingerings before you begin.

3. **Look out for accidentals.** Check that you know the fingering before you arrive at the note.

4. **Look for patterns.** While tapping the rhythm, look at the melodic shape and notice movement by step, skips, repeated notes and sequences.

5. **Notice the articulation and dynamics.**

6. **Keep going!**

Performance directions used in Section 6
(Note these on the glossary page at the back of the book)

Cantilena – a song-like melody
Capricioso – capricious
Con energia – with energy
Grazioso – gracefully
Pomposo – pompously
Scherzando – in a playful manner

A partir de maintenant vous devrez déterminer la tonalité vous-même

Six étapes vers la réussite

1. **Observez l'indication de mesure.** Frappez (dans les mains, chantez ou jouez sur une seule note) le *rythme* tout en maintenant une pulsation intérieure constante. Comptez mentalement au moins une mesure pour installer la pulsation avant de frapper le rythme ou de jouer la pièce.

2. **Vérifiez les dièses ou les bémols placés entre la clef de *sol* et l'indication de mesure.** Ils constituent l'armure de la tonalité. Assurez vous des notes altérées et repérez-les dans la mélodie. Pensez aux doigtés avant de commencer.

3. **Recherchez les altérations accidentelles.** Contrôlez votre doigté avant d'atteindre la note.

4. **Repérez les motifs.** Tout en frappant le rythme, observez les contours de la mélodie et relevez les mouvements par degré, les sauts d'intervalles, les notes répétées et les séquences.

5. **Observez le phrasé et les nuances.**

6. **Ne vous arrêtez pas !**

Indications d'exécution utilisées dans cette section
(à inscrire sur la page de glossaire en fin de volume)

Cantilena – cantilène
Capricioso – capricieux
Con energia – avec énergie
Grazioso – gracieux
Pomposo – pompeux
Scherzando – en badinant

Von jetzt an musst du selbst entscheiden, um welche Taktart es sich handelt.

Sechs Schritte zum Erfolg

1. **Schaue dir die Taktangabe an.** Schlage (klatsche, singe oder spiele auf einer Note) den *Rhythmus*, wobei du immer das Metrum spürst. Zähle mindestens einen Takt lang die Taktangabe im Kopf, um das Metrum zu verinnerlichen, bevor du jede der Melodien klopfst oder spielst.

2. **Achte auf Kreuz- und B- Vorzeichen zwischen dem Notenschlüssel und der Taktangabe.** Versichere dich, dass du weißt, auf welche Noten sich diese beziehen und finde heraus, wo in der Melodie sie auftauchen. Überprüfe ihre Griffweise, bevor du zu spielen anfängst.

3. **Suche nach Notenvorzeichen.** Stelle sicher, dass du die Griffweise kennst, bevor du diese Note erreichst.

4. **Achte auf Muster.** Schaue dir die melodische Form an, während du den Rhythmus schlägst und achte auf Bewegungen in Schritten oder Sprüngen, sich wiederholende Noten und Sequenzen.

5. **Beachte Artikulation und Dynamik.**

6. **Bleibe dran!**

Vortragsangaben für den Teil 6
(Notiere diese auf der entsprechenden Seite im Glossar)

Cantilena – eine liedhafte Melodie
Capricioso – launenhaft
Con energia – mit Energie
Grazioso – anmutig
Pomposo – feierlich
Scherzando – auf spielerische Art und Weise

Section 6 – The upper (clarinet) register
Section 6 – Le registre supérieur (clairon)
Teil 6 – Das obere (Klarinetten-) Register

Notes C – G   Notes: *do* à *sol*   Die Noten c" – g"

New note A   Nouvelle note: *la*   Die neue Note a"

119.

Flowing

120.

Allegretto

121.

Allegretto

New note F♯.
Look out for syncopated rhythm ♪ ♩ ♪

Nouvelle note: *fa* ♯
Attention au rythme syncopé ♪ ♩ ♪

Die neue Note fis". Achte auf den
Synkopen-Rhythmus ♪ ♩ ♪

122.

Scherzando

Look out for syncopated rhythm

Attention au ryhme syncopé

Achte auf den Synkopen-Rhythmus

123.

New note C♯

Nouvelle note *do* ♯

Neue Note cis"

124.

125.

126.

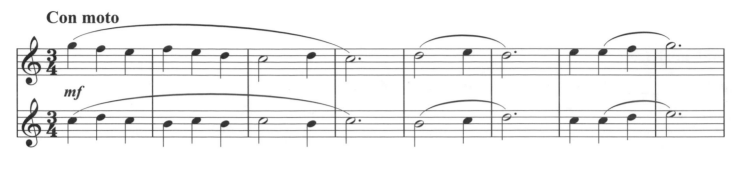

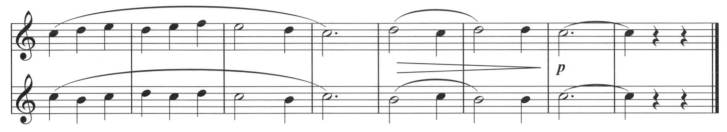

127.

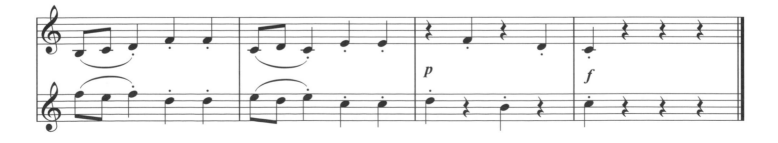

128.

129.

Grazioso

130.

Con energia

131.

Cantilena

Section 7 – Joining the chalumeau and clarinet registers
Section 7 – Relier les registres de chalumeau et de clairon
Teil 7 – Das Chalumeau- und Klarinetten-Register werden miteinander verbunden

Seven steps to success

1. **Look at the time signature.** Tap (clap, sing or play on one note) the *rhythm,* feeling the pulse throughout. Count at least one bar of the time signature in your head to set up the pulse before you tap or play each tune.

2. **Look between the treble clef and the time signature for any sharps or flats.** Make sure you know which notes these apply to and notice where they occur in the melody. Sort out the fingerings before you begin.

3. **Look out for accidentals.** Check that you know the fingering before you arrive at the note.

4. **Work out how to cross the 'break'.** Decide which little fingers to use before you start. This is most important in D major, B minor, E minor and D minor. Check whether accidentals influence the little finger patterns.

5. **Look for patterns.** While tapping the rhythm, look at the melodic shape and notice movement by step, skips, repeated notes and sequences.

6. **Notice the articulation and dynamics.**

7. **Keep going!**

New Performance directions used in Section 7
(Note these on the glossary page at the back of the book)

Largamente – broadly
Più mosso – faster
Ritmico – rhythmically

Sept étapes vers la réussite

1. **Observez l'indication de mesure.** Frappez (dans les mains, chantez ou jouez sur une seule note) le *rythme* tout en maintenant une pulsation intérieure constante. Comptez mentalement au moins une mesure pour installer la pulsation avant de frapper le rythme ou de jouer la pièce.

2. **Vérifiez les dièses ou les bémols placés entre la clef de *sol* et l'indication de mesure.** Ils constituent l'armure de la tonalité. Assurez vous des notes altérées et repérez-les dans la mélodie. Pensez aux doigtés avant de commencer.

3. **Recherchez les altérations accidentelles.** Contrôlez votre doigté avant d'atteindre la note.

4. **Travaillez le « passage » d'un registre à l'autre.** Déterminer l'annulaire à utiliser avant de commencer. Ceci est très important en *ré* majeur, *si* mineur, *mi* mineur et *ré* mineur. Vérifiez si les altérations modifient les positions de l'annulaire.

5. **Repérez les motifs.** Tout en frappant le rythme, observez les contours de la mélodie et relevez les mouvements par degré, les sauts d'intervalles, les notes répétées et les séquences.

6. **Observez le phrasé et les nuances.**

7. **Ne vous arrêtez pas !**

Indications d'exécution utilisées dans cette section
(à inscrire sur la page de glossaire en fin de volume)

Largamente – largement
Più mosso – plus vite
Ritmico – rythmé

Sieben Schritte zum Erfolg

1. **Schaue dir die Taktangabe an.** Schlage (klatsche, singe oder spiele auf einer Note) den *Rhythmus*, wobei du immer das Metrum spürst. Zähle mindestens einen Takt lang die Taktangabe im Kopf, um das Metrum zu verinnerlichen, bevor du jede der Melodien klopfst oder spielst.

2. **Achte auf Kreuz- und B- Vorzeichen zwischen dem Notenschlüssel und der Taktangabe.** Versichere dich, dass du weißt, auf welche Noten sich diese beziehen und finde heraus, wo in der Melodie sie auftauchen. Überprüfe ihre Griffweise, bevor du zu spielen anfängst.

3. **Suche nach Notenvorzeichen.** Stelle sicher, dass du die Griffweise kennst, bevor du diese Note erreichst.

4. **Lege vorher fest, wie du den ‚Übergang' überbrückst.** Entscheide dich vor dem Spielen, welche kleinen Finger du benutzen wirst. Besonders wichtig ist das bei den Tonarten D-Dur, B-Moll, E-Moll und D-Moll. Überprüfe, ob irgendwelche Vorzeichen deine Überlegungen für die kleinen Finger beeinflussen.

5. **Achte auf Muster.** Schaue dir die melodische Form an, während du den Rhythmus schlägst und achte auf Bewegungen in Schritten oder Sprüngen, sich wiederholende Noten und Sequenzen.

6. **Beachte Artikulation und Dynamik.**

7. **Bleibe dran!**

Neue Vortragsangaben für den Teil 7
(Notiere diese auf der entsprechenden Seite im Glossar)

Largamente – breit
Più mosso – schneller
Ritmico – rhythmisch

Section 7 – Joining the chalumeau and clarinet registers

Section 7 – Relier les registres de chalumeau et de clairon

Teil 7 – Das Chalumeau- und Klarinetten-Register werden miteinander verbunden

132.

133.

134.

135.

136.

Capriccioso

137.

Lullaby

138.

Allegro

139.

140.

141.

142.

143.

Animato

144.

Allegro

Largamente   Più mosso

145.

Moderato

146.

Vivace

rit.

62

147.

Allegro con brio

148.

Andantino

149.

Con moto

150.

Presto

151.

Moderato

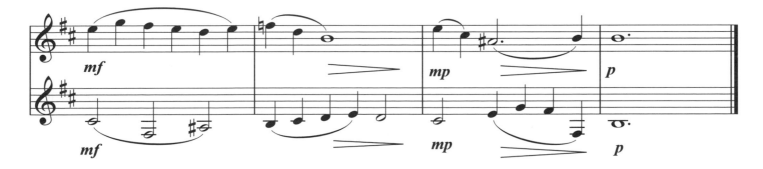

152.

Andantino

153.

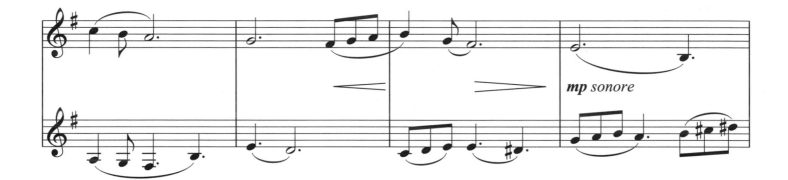

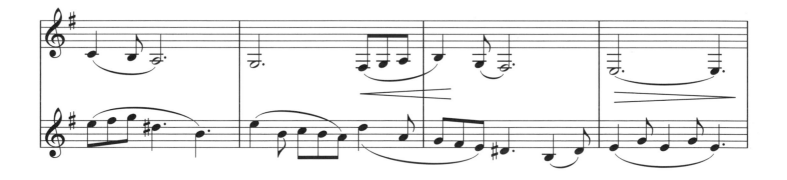

154.

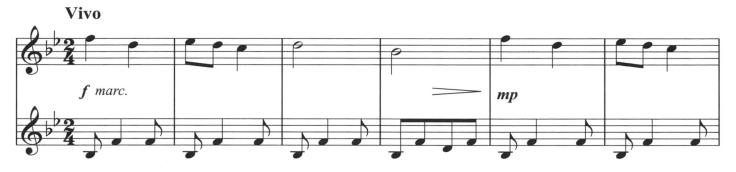

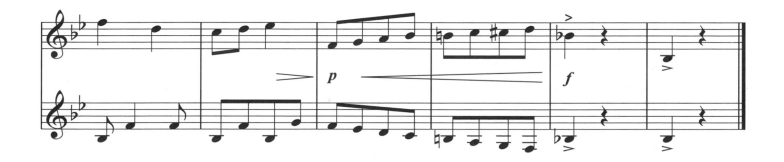

155.

156.

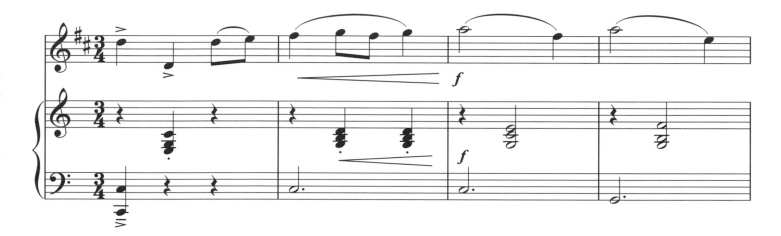

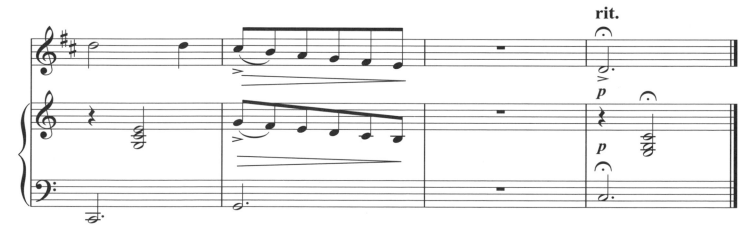

157.

Andante con moto

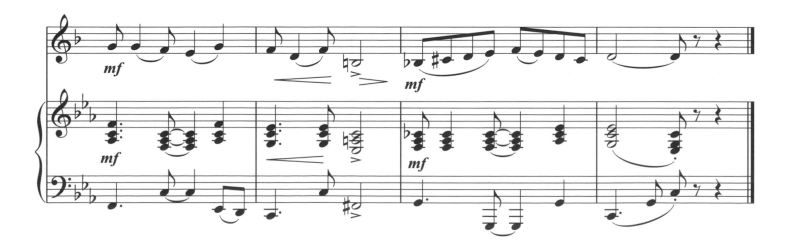

Glossary
Glossaire
Glossar

Note performance directions together with their translations used throughout the book so that you have a complete list. Writing them down will help you to remember them.

Inscrivez ici les indications d'exécution utilisées dans ce volume et leur traduction pour en établir une liste complète. Le fait de les noter vous aidera à les retenir.

Notiere hier alle Vortragsangaben, die in diesem Buch benutzt werden, zusammen mit ihren Übersetzungen, so dass du eine vollständige Liste hast. Das Aufschreiben wird dir dabei helfen, sie dir einzuprägen.

Adagio	slowly	lent	langsam
